I KNOW WHY

God's Gracious Gift of Trials

by Keri Foutz Cottrell

Some trials are big

And some are small

But with God's help

We'll conquer all.

-KFC

Dedication

To my husband - for supporting my dreams and always being there for me, come what may. I couldn't have done it without you – my knight in shining armor.

To my parents and siblings - for your amazing examples of service, dedication to the Lord, and faith through innumerable trials. Crazy adventures were more fun with ten of us! What a great cheering squad you are!

To my Heavenly Father and Jesus Christ - for my life, my hope, and the promise of peace. I am so grateful to all those who have dedicated their lives to providing us with more of Your divine words through scripture and revelation. I am so thankful to be a member of the Church of Jesus Christ of Latter-day Saints where so many opportunities for growth and eternal understanding are available.

Acknowledgements

I must thank my siblings and children for providing so much to write about and still leaving me sane enough to write it. Thank you for also bringing so much joy into my life: so much more meaningful because there was sorrow and peace.

Thanks to all those who let me bounce my ideas around and helped me finally get this on the page through inspiration, reading and edits. Support is so vital! Big hugs to you all!

Table of Contents

Introduction

*But behold, I, Nephi, will show unto you that
the tender mercies of the Lord are over all those
whom he hath chosen, because of their faith, to
make them mighty even unto the power of
deliverance. (1 Nephi 1:20)*

———

A bold title, I know. It took many decades
of life to figure this out, but I firmly believe God
loves us so much and is so dedicated in doing all
possible to ensure the success of our mission here
on earth (so that we may return to Him), that
through tough love and tender mercies, He
allows those experiences (difficult as they may be)
that will ensure our victory.

The whole idea came to me while watching
a movie. I love action-packed films where the
hero is faced with insurmountable odds, defeat
looks certain, and he or she achieves victory
anyway. Wouldn't we all like to be heroes like
that? I must say, I think we are: if you are reading
this now, you have already overcome many
things and will probably face more, but with the
ultimate power in the universe on our side, how
can any of us fail? That's what this book is about:
looking at the obstacles of life from a completely

different perspective—an eternal perspective—that will change your view and attitude in unimaginable ways.

In the particular film that changed my outlook, a leader chose someone for a challenging task who had just endured a difficult physical rehabilitation, knowing that overcoming hardship in one area meant good chances for success in another. I was struck by the thought that this might be Heavenly Father's perspective as well: is He determined to prepare us for what lies ahead—whatever it takes? Could it be possible that like a drill sergeant, He gives us challenges and allows trials that will strengthen the skills we need to successfully overcome future events that might be even more difficult? What if situations we think of as hard or terrible are actually the benevolent 'inoculations' we need to handle what is coming next? Although religions often focus on the tender mercies of God, the scriptures are full of references to his 'tough love' approach as well. Pondering this question, I wondered if there might be any examples in the scriptures. I was overwhelmed by the evidence.

In the beginning, Heavenly Father warned Adam and Eve about the difficulties of earth life.

Enoch is encouraged to be a prophet despite his speech issues and unpopularity and in a very sinful environment and inspires many to become a Zion people God raises up to heaven.

Abraham is rescued by an angel from being sacrificed; flees his home to wander the middle east witnessing many evidences of God's power; is promised a son; waits decades for that promise to be fulfilled; and then is tested to see if he will sacrifice that son to God.

Joseph of Egypt went through repeated trials: constantly succeeding and then being set back—from favored son to lowly slave; from running Potiphar's house to jail—before becoming a powerful ruler in Egypt.

Another example is Moses. He was prepared in the court of Pharaoh with the knowledge of the language and protocols and then in the desert with the faith and power he would eventually need to achieve the release of the Israelite nation.

Protecting his sheep from predators enabled David to later face Goliath and other enemies with courage and faith that would inspire a nation.

Daniel's many challenges as a prophet and statesman in Babylon--requesting simple foods, interpreting Nebuchadnezzar's dreams, knowing his friends were rescued from the furnace-- certainly helped Daniel know the Lord would be with him in the lion's den. And more importantly, his excellent example paved the way for Babylonian kings to be kind to future Jewish courtiers: enabling Queen Esther to save the Jewish people from destruction and Nehemiah to rebuild Jerusalem.

Examples are not only found within *The Holy Bible*. *The Book of Mormon* also reveals how the Lord strengthened people through trials. Didn't Nephi's success retrieving the plates from Laban [being *"led by the Spirit, not knowing beforehand the things which [he] should do" (1st Nephi 4:6)*] give him confidence to build a ship worthy of crossing an unknown ocean, relying alone upon the Lord's instructions? Or to later follow the Lord's direction to break away from the main group in a strange new land and carve out a better life?

Alma's personal conversion certainly added more faith to his prayers for his son. Knowing the thrall of a wicked life as one of King Noah's priests and that revelation of a holier way and repentance could change a person forever was valuable to Alma as he hoped and prayed the same would happen for his son, Alma the younger.

I am sure you can recall many stories of other prophets and famous people who have endured hardships along the road that culminated in the fulfillment of their ultimate achievements and sometimes fame.

In reminiscing, I see that my previous trials prepared me for success as an adult: the stumbling blocks in my early years became the stepping stones I needed to fortify me so I could endure and even conquer what lay ahead. Like the chick is strengthened by its struggle from the egg, our challenges toughen us up for what lies ahead — and I have seen many examples of this in my own life.

Chapter 1: FAMILY

*And behold, I tell you these things that ye may
learn wisdom; that ye may learn that when ye
are in the service of your fellow beings ye are
only in the service of your God. (Mosiah 2:17)*

Besides King Benjamin who taught his
family and people principles like the one above,
many *Book of Mormon* prophets taught their
children to turn to God for wisdom and support
and to serve others.

*Behold, it came to pass that I, Enos, knowing my
father that he was a just man — for he taught me
in his language, and also in the nurture and
admonition of the Lord — and blessed be the name
of my God for it — and I will tell you of
the wrestle which I had before God, before I
received a remission of my sins. Behold, I went to
hunt beasts in the forests; and the words which I
had often heard my father speak concerning
eternal life, and the joy of the saints, sunk deep
into my heart. (Enos 1:1-3)*

I was raised in a large family full of strong personalities. We laughed and played, studied and sang, worked and wrestled. We were loud but loving and I count myself extremely blessed to have siblings who genuinely care for each other and don't take offense or assume the worst when things come up or awkward words are said. Although not perfect, my parents passed on an amazing legacy of self-worth, spirituality, and service that inspires us daily. They truly loved us, encouraged us to believe in ourselves, fostered our various talents, and attended our innumerable concerts, games, and performances. They carved out time for spiritual opportunities and service so we could see outside of ourselves and learn God's great plan for us. It wasn't easy or always fun, but the wonderful results I see in my own life and my siblings' have helped me as a parent to continue on faithfully. My parents' faith, patience, love and determination to follow church leaders' counsel was also inspiring. Because of my upbringing, I know that attending church; reading scriptures; enjoying quality family time; giving honest praise, lots of hugs and service to others will transform messy, sassy, energetic children into amazing, effective adults who love the Lord and their families and serve with all their hearts.

One of the easiest examples is family scripture study. A few years after my sister and I were born, a few rowdy boys joined the family in quick succession. They made many things more difficult than when there had only been two responsible girls to account for. Family home evening and scripture time became a circus — a three ring circus in fact! Through the years, however, I saw the words of the Lord begin to sink in and each of them eventually received a testimony of their own regarding the truthfulness of the scriptures (and the ability to sit still). Currently they are all inspirational leaders in their homes, churches and businesses. The amazing men I am fortunate to call my brothers are incredible transformations of the whirling dervishes they were as children. I have also seen the same transformation in my own home. So, carry on with attempts at spiritual instruction with young children--I know there is hope.

Another fond memory is Christmas caroling in the rain. Where we grew up, the winter holidays were signaled by frequent rain. Inevitably, the nights chosen to visit friends and neighbors with cookies and caroling were some of the wettest. As a teen, I was incensed that I had to leave the comfort of my warm home and a good book, to go perform for a person I barely knew. Why disturb their hard-earned quiet with our music and spoil their diets with more sugar? I could always invent many reasons not to go, but we always went.

Although we had many amazing experiences — and still do now when any of us are together at Christmas — I remember one night in particular. It was a few days before Christmas and rain had been pouring down all day: everything was wet and soggy and large puddles lurked in the darkness. We had visited a few neighbors and had one more to go. I was wet, had cold feet, was tired of being squished in the back seat with squirmy siblings and just wanted to get back home and dry off. The dingy apartment complex we stopped at was dark and cramped, but at least our prospective audience was on the ground floor. When the frail door opened and the sweet face of one of the widows in our congregation peeked out, I was surprised by the hope and happiness in her countenance. As we began to sing and handed her the plate of cookies, I felt the most amazing peace and compassion. Even now…many decades later…I am struck with the love I felt for her and the understanding that sharing gifts of song and treats were more important than extra time reading my book. Most important of all was that she felt remembered and cared for. Later, my father told me that she had no children or family and that our yearly Christmas visits were some of her most cherished memories.

Previews are the best — helping us see what is coming and how it can be dealt with. The experiences I had growing up helped me have more patience with my own kids. The best part has been seeing my own children affected in the same way as we have passed these traditions on. Washington state is almost as rainy as Hawaii and the nights we found for caroling were usually wet. My children complained as I had as a teen and were hesitant to leave the warmth for people they hardly knew. Although it took a few years, my children eventually began to look forward to this activity, and they have noticed the light in the eyes of friends as we bless them with carols and cookies. I remember the night we visited a widower in his small house at the edge of a dark forest where we always had to wade through a crowd of large barking dogs (don't let them see fear, kids!) to get to his front door. We had just moved to a new congregation and when he saw us at the door, he began to cry, saying "I didn't think you would come this year, but was sure hoping you would." Even my teenagers were moved by this display of joy and finally understood the importance of our visits. On the way home, they actually expressed happiness at being able to share their talents with others and said it was worth braving the cold weather and intimidating dogs. Complaints of 'do we have to?' have been replaced with 'who are we caroling next?' and the harmony is healing to all.

Chapter 2: CHILDHOOD

*Withhold not thou thy tender mercies from me,
O L*ORD*: let thy lovingkindness and thy truth
continually preserve me. (Psalms 40:11)*

————

Jacob often felt like the 'odd man out' in his family. His Dad and brother both loved hunting and he was more of a scholar. When family conflict required that he leave home, he went with the Lord's blessing to live with relatives in a country far away. Holding fast to his faith and with guidance from the Lord, Jacob was prosperous despite his uncle Laban's deceptions and eventually returned home with 4 wives, 12 children and a lot of striped sheep.

*And Jacob vowed a vow, saying, If God will be
with me, and will keep me in this way that I go,
and will give me bread to eat, and raiment to put
on, so that I come again to my father's house in
peace; then shall the L*ORD *be my God. (Genesis
28:20-21)*

————

My childhood memories are not all good ones. My parents were great, my Mom stayed home to care for and nurture us, we always had food on the table and clothes to wear (often secondhand or homemade), but the area I grew up in was a bit rough. I especially did not fit in at school. I was a minority, large for my age, and unlike my classmates, excited to learn all I could. Many of the children came from difficult environments where English was not spoken and parents were gone, or abusive. In fact, some were raised by grandparents and felt cast off. I did not realize this until many years later.

Oblivious to the difficulties of the other kids, I could not understand why they were not as excited about school or as happy about my success as my parents were. Over the years I realized that only my family cared that I had done well on a test; others were mad I had raised the grading curve. Coming from broken homes or suffering from absent parents, they felt I was bragging when I talked about reading lots of books and playing games with my family after school.

Besides my awkward social issues, being a minority could be a dangerous thing where I grew up. It took me awhile to realize it would be better to keep to myself. I learned that lesson the hard way when one of my few friends was badly hurt. In kindergarten, Paul *(name changed)* and I would 'drive' the playground firetruck, imagining we were winning battles against large fires. As often as possible we would race out to recess to be the first ones in the drivers' seats. On a day I will never forget--when someone else took command of the engine first—we chose to play on the jungle gym. I am not sure what started the skirmish--maybe someone felt we were encroaching on their playground 'territory'--but some native kids began throwing rocks at Paul and he was hit so many times that he fell off the jungle gym and had to be rushed to the hospital. I still recall seeing him fall--blood trickling down his head--and being taken away in the ambulance. I never saw him again.

During my remaining years at that school, I was pinched and teased—slowly and painfully learning to keep my love of school to myself. My 3rd grade teacher did not know how to help kids from different races and levels of learning get along and usually just gave me the job of tutoring the same kids who were bullying me, which just made it worse. Although my parents did their best to encourage me, school was hard for a smart kid who was slow to learn tact.

The next year my family thankfully moved to a new area of town where I could attend a different school. The teachers there encouraged everyone: nurturing and challenging all the students at their different levels of ability instead of highlighting differences or allowing bullying. Although I often still felt awkward and spent a lot of my time alone reading in the library during recess, I began to make new friends. I found a new group to hang out with on the playground and replaced imaginary firefighting with space adventures.

As I reached high school, I realized more fully that socially I was not as 'in tune' as the others. I could achieve whatever came my way educationally, but understanding why my friends acted the way they did was a puzzle. I found a few friends who shared my same values and didn't have a hidden agenda I was always trying to guess at and did my best to endure the teen years. Band, choir, and drama classes helped me to blend in better and find friends who had my same interests.

Decades later--when my one of my sons was diagnosed with Asperger's--I realized I was a bit on the 'spectrum' too. People with Asperger's learn anything that interests them very quickly, but social skills — reading others' emotions and deciphering relationship clues — are not as easy. Thankfully science has figured much of this out recently, so my husband and I were able to find some therapies and coaching to help our son succeed more fully. We also encouraged him to keep his successes to himself unless others asked. We made sure he knew that we were proud of his stellar achievements, but reminded him that others might be less thrilled or consider it bragging. We prompted him to find a few good friends, enjoy his studies, and not worry about the rest of the craziness, social whims and pressure to be a certain way at school. (And we lived in a safer part of the country where people with different racial backgrounds lived more harmoniously.)

Like Jacob learned successful skills to survive in a strange land and taught them to his son, Joseph, so he could figure out success in Egypt, I was able to pass on my experience and knowledge to my son. Having navigated a life with Asperger's, I knew my son could handle it too. Although it hasn't been easy, and still has challenges for both of us, I know my experiences made it a bit easier for him.

Chapter 3: FRIENDS

Thou shalt love thy neighbor as thyself. (Mark 12:31)

———

Was Alma's faith in his son's eventual change of heart more hopeful because he had gone through the same thing: turned from wicked choices to a dedicated ministry? Knowing personally that Christ could affect such a drastic change must have encouraged his prayers for those many years. Later, Alma the younger gives an account to his son, Helaman in Alma, chapter 36, verses 1-9 (*underline added*):

My son, give ear to my words; for I swear unto you, that inasmuch as ye shall keep the commandments of God ye shall prosper in the land. I would that ye should do as I have done, in remembering the captivity of our fathers; for they were in bondage, and none could deliver them except it was the God of Abraham, and the God of Isaac, and the God of Jacob; and he surely did deliver them in their afflictions. And now, O my son Helaman, behold, thou art in thy youth, and therefore, I beseech of thee that thou wilt hear my words and learn of me; for I do know that whosoever shall put their trust in God shall be supported

22

*in their trials, and their troubles, and their
afflictions, and shall be lifted up at the last day.
And I would not that ye think that I know of
myself — not of the temporal but of the spiritual,
not of the carnal mind but of God. Now, behold,
I say unto you, if I had not been born of God, I
should not have known these things; but God
has, by the mouth of his holy angel, made these
things known unto me, not of
any worthiness of myself; For I went about
with the sons of Mosiah, seeking to destroy the
church of God; but behold, God sent his holy
angel to stop us by the way. And behold, he
spake unto us, as it were the voice of thunder,
and the whole earth did tremble beneath our
feet; and we all fell to the earth, for the fear of
the Lord came upon us. But behold, the voice
said unto me: Arise. And I arose and stood up,
and beheld the angel. And he said unto me: If
thou wilt of thyself be destroyed, seek no more
to destroy the church of God.*

After recounting his conversion story —
spurred by the memory of his father's testimony
of the Savior's healing power and ability to
forgive--Alma continues:

*Yea, and from that time even until now, I have
labored without ceasing, that I might bring
souls unto repentance; that I might bring them
to taste of the exceeding joy of which I did
taste; that they might also be born of God, and
be filled with the Holy Ghost….And I have*

been supported under trials and troubles of
every kind, yea, and in all manner of
afflictions; yea, God has delivered me from
prison, and from bonds, and from death; yea,
and I do put my trust in him, and he will
still deliver me. (Alma 36:24-27, underline
added)

———

Not that we all expect an angelic visit for those who are straying from correct life choices, but learning to love people as they are, positively reminding them of who they can become, and praying for God to fill in the spaces can help as we wait for that mighty change.

My father taught me that respect for everyone is vital. His job required that he interact with people from a variety of cultures and economic situations. We lived in an area full of wealthy and poor from all over the world, and he showed me that Christ-like love for everyone was possible. He advised that we never judge others for their circumstances, but instead learn about their lives and show kindness. He told us everyone had a history that explained why they lived the way they did and acted in certain ways: tragic losses, amazing fortune, difficult childhoods, varying cultures, and different health concerns had shaped their attitudes and lives. Watching my father treat everyone he met with respect and genuine interest--whether humble, handicapped, rich or famous — taught me to do this in my own life.

Because of his example, my life is richer through friends from many different countries, religions, and economic backgrounds. I love talking to people wherever I go and discovering their history. This ability also helped me overcome my childhood shyness — knowing that everyone has a story and that when we know more about them, we can be patient, kind, and understand their actions better. During high school many of my friends were lonely and felt abandoned by parents through divorce, illness, busy social lives, or work. Although they were sometimes overwhelmed when I brought them home to meet my big family of ten (a rare sight, especially in Hawaii), they were later inspired by the joy and fun they saw there. I know some of them later strived to create that atmosphere when they eventually formed families of their own.

I remember a few friends in high school who turned to drinking, pain killers or drugs to alleviate the discomfort of their difficult home lives. As I watched them struggle with self-worth issues, I did all I could to help them realize how amazing and talented they were. I tried to remind them that chemicals would not solve their problems, but mess up their lives in other ways.

My father's example of charity and the diversity of my high school friends prepared me to love and nurture the son we were able to adopt. Although he came to our home soon after he was born, we were constantly surprised by his actions, attitudes, and ideas. Nurturing can help shape a person, but their innate nature will always be a factor. We focused on the positive, provided lots of different opportunities for him to find his strengths, and taught him all we could to prepare him for life ahead.

When our son decided to try drugs and alcohol to cover up his feelings of despair from bad choices he had made, we continued to love and encourage him, reminding him of all the good in his life. Sometimes he became so mired in his bad situation that he threatened or attempted suicide. These moments were particularly dark and saddening, but as our family prayed for him, we always felt peace, were inspired about what to say, and things worked out okay. Although he has curtailed many of his habits, his life is still not easy. Like I did with my friends in high school, I continue to remind him of how amazing he is and that he has the power to shape his future in positive ways. He is now married with a son and although he still struggles at times, he knows there is a God who has the power to forgive and provide strength through the hard times. He has also thanked us for raising him with good core values and teaching him about God.

Learning to love and accept all of his diversity has been easier because of the example my father provided and the high school friends I met: to be patient, love others despite their choices, and look for the best in all. I realize now how Heavenly Father is sorrowful when we stray, but loves us anyway. The eternal perspective enables us to understand how this life is but an instant, and that there is so much more to everything than one small moment or action. I feel so fortunate to have been given many heavenly reassurances that God loves our son and our family, knows our difficulties, and generously provides us with the *"peace that passeth all understanding." (Philippians 4:7)*

Chapter 4: SCHOOL

*And not only so, but we glory in tribulations
also: knowing that tribulation worketh patience;
and patience, experience; and experience, hope:
and hope maketh not ashamed; because the love
of God is shed abroad in our hearts by the Holy
Ghose which is given unto us. (Romans 5:3-5)*

———

When we read the story of Moses, we are
often saddened by the realization that except for a
few years with his mother as nursemaid, he was
separated from his family and religious
traditions. We know that his placement at the
palace of Pharaoh certainly saved his life, but
"desperate times called for desperate measures"
and Moses needed extraordinary preparation for
his incredible venture ahead. By spending his
childhood in the Egyptian courts--learning
protocols, leadership, traditions, and languages,
Moses was prepared to eventually return to those
same courts to confront Pharaoh and demand the
release of the Israelite nation. His exile in the
desert equipped him to lead the children of Israel
through future wastelands. The Lord revealed his
power to Moses through a burning bush
unconsumed and a leprous hand returned to
health, fortifying him with confidence that in the

future, exodus from Egypt, dry passage through the Red Sea, and heavenly manna would be possible.

> *And Israel saw that great work which the LORD did upon the Egyptians: and the people feared the LORD, and believed the LORD, and his servant Moses. (Exodus 14:31)*

———

Where I lived, the secondary public schools could be brutal and the teachers had a very difficult time controlling student behavior. It was much safer and academically wiser to attend one of the many private schools in the area. Schools associated with a religion were often more reasonably priced and so, after elementary school, I had a chance to attend one close to home. I thrived in the disciplined and faith-based environment. The classes were small; the teachers were able to impart their knowledge without combatting rowdy behavior; the atmosphere was calm and nurturing; and even the science teachers acknowledged God and his love for us. However, the religion was different than mine, and it took some time to find friends I could discuss scriptures with and not have it devolve into '*Bible* bashing.' Eventually, I found some who truly honored God in their lives and we were able to discuss spiritual experiences; share our love of the scriptures; and respect one another's ideas. Another difficult aspect of school was that we were tested on the tenets of the Lutheran religion. As a good student, I memorized what was required so I could pass the tests, but wrote my essays quickly so I could then mention what I believed that was different. Attending the Church of Jesus Christ of Latter-day Saints' early morning seminary program before school also gave me knowledge of the Old and New Testaments of *The Bible* that helped as well.

A hallmark memory occurred at high school graduation, when many of them commented to me about how amazed and inspired they were that I had not just talked about my faith in God and the scriptures, but had actually lived the commandments throughout the years. They then shared how they wished they had been as true to God and their beliefs. I was shocked: I had not realized they were watching me so closely. I was glad to find out that I had been a positive role model by not drinking alcohol or smoking; walking out of a movie I should not have taken a chance on; not being immoral; and speaking up about the surety of my beliefs.

When the Church of Jesus Christ of Latter-day Saints asked me to serve a mission to a country where my high school's same religion was dominant, I realized what a tender mercy my high school experiences had been. Visiting with the people of Denmark, I was comfortable discussing Christ and his gospel while reinforcing the commonalities between our faiths, just like I had in high school. People are much more willing to discuss difficult topics like religion when they feel understood and acknowledged. Throughout my mission, I felt very blessed to be able to understand others' religious points of view and address their questions. Although it had been challenging to go to a school administrated by another religion, I felt very blessed that those experiences--as difficult as they were--enabled me to better serve in a country where I was already familiar with their concepts of God and faith.

I can see now that it was truly a tender mercy — in many ways – to attend Our Redeemer Lutheran school. I was so blessed to have amazing teachers who treated me kindly and were able to mention God and his profound influence on the world around us. Although it was uncomfortable to stand up for my beliefs that were different (while trying not to offend or negate someone else's), I learned valuable skills I would need for the future. I also learned to value and respect others' personal faith although different from my own and I count myself lucky to still have many friends of other faiths.

Chapter 5: LOSS & GAIN

For my thoughts are not your thoughts, neither
are your ways my ways, saith the Lord. For
as the heavens are higher than the earth, so are
my ways higher than your ways, and
my thoughts than your thoughts. (Isaiah 55:8-9)

———

"Then gentle Mary meekly bowed her head
'To me be as it pleaseth God,' she said,
'My soul shall laud and magnify His holy
name.'"

———

A few years after I was married, I heard
this Christmas carol on the radio. A popular artist
had released a rendition of it and the words of
Gabriel's message to the virgin Mary struck me
with great force. The thought came that if Mary
was willing to follow God's plan for her life and
risk death to have a child, I should be willing to
be without children if that was His plan for me.
After many years of marriage, I felt so awkward
to be in congregations full of children and have
none. The phrase, *"To me be as it pleaseth God"*,
was profound and I felt as if He was speaking to
me when I heard the words. I realized that I
should be thankful for my life exactly as it was,

and that my present and future were in God's hands. A later priesthood blessing from my husband reassured me that God had his own timing and that someday I would be a mother.

Although I continued to visit specialists and try different remedies, medicines, diets and therapies, it took a while to discover the problem. One solution was injectable fertility drugs and though I got pregnant, I was allergic to one of the drugs used. I became very ill (including fluid gathering in my lungs) and eventually miscarried. This was a very depressing episode in my life and my faith in God was shaken. I could not fathom why when all I wanted was to be a mother, this child had not survived. Patiently my husband encouraged me to not give up on the Lord, but to start praying again for peace. I followed his advice and over time my body, mind and spirit began to heal. I realized many years later that these feelings were mostly a result of postpartum depression and the extra pregnancy hormones that were in the fertility drugs.

Not wanting to risk my life again, we decided to adopt and were fortunate to be chosen quickly to receive a baby boy. We were excited to be parents and although it was challenging, I continued to look into ways that my body might heal so that we might add more children to our family. I was inspired to visit a therapist who helped me deal with some past issues that were actually preventing my fertility. Over time researchers discovered other remedies for my medical issue and, at the age most friends were done having children, I was able to begin and we were blessed with a few more children in our home.

I was so thankful to the Lord for finally giving me children, that much of my perspective on parenting was changed. I even called their dirty diapers 'presents', reasoning that if I didn't have children, I wouldn't have dirty diapers to deal with. (Although as the oldest of 8 children I had changed my allotment of dirty diapers, I was thrilled to have more.) I believe I was more patient with the difficulties of parenting because I waited so many years for my children to arrive. Now that decades have passed--filled with many wonderful revelations from the Lord regarding my desires for motherhood--I can see that my plans needed to wait for God's timing of when my children were to arrive on earth. As usual, peace and fulfillment come by trusting in his plans and not leaning unto our own understanding (*Proverbs 3:5*).

Chapter 6: ILLNESS

Behold, we count them happy which endure.
(James 5:11)

———

A prophet named Alma from *The Book of Mormon* started his preaching career persuading people to turn away from Christ, and like Saul (whose name was changed to Paul in the New Testament of *The Holy Bible*), later became a powerful missionary after an angel's visit.

…I cried within my heart: O Jesus, thou Son of God, have mercy on me, who am in the gall of bitterness, and am encircled about by the everlasting chains of death. And now, behold, when I thought this, I could remember my pains no more; yea, I was harrowed up by the memory of my sins no more. And oh, what joy, and what marvelous light I did behold; yea, my soul was filled with joy as exceeding as was my pain! (Alma 36:18-20)

Later Alma meets a lawyer named Zeezrom who spends his life causing contention to create clients. After Zeezrom is caught in his lies and recognizes God but becomes ill with a fever brought on by the torment of sin, Alma knows he can be healed as well.

> *And then Alma cried unto the Lord, saying: O*
> *Lord our God, have mercy on this man,*
> *and heal him according to his faith which is in*
> *Christ. And when Alma had said these*
> *words, Zeezrom leaped upon his feet, and began*
> *to walk…(Alma 15:10-11)*

———

Although not quite the same as burning fevers caused by sin against God, susceptibility to respiratory illness runs in my family. Many of my siblings had respiratory issues as babies: croup, whooping cough, and asthma. As the oldest in a large family, I recall many instances of sitting in a steamy bathroom with a fussy toddler encouraging them to breathe deeply. A few times I even accompanied my mom to the hospital so they could be treated with steroids or other medications. One of my clearest memories was trying to distract an 18-month-old sister in the hospital with Christmas tv shows so she wouldn't remove the IV from her foot while our mom took a break to go to church.

All of this experience helped me immensely when only five weeks after birth, one of my children contracted RSV--a respiratory virus especially dangerous for infants. Thinking at first that it was just a bit of a cold, my husband

and I were surprised when the symptoms worsened, and understandably shaken when we saw that breathing was difficult. Into the steamy bathroom we went, applying saline to the nose and menthol to the chest, but soon the infant became unconscious and it took a brisk chest massage to inspire breathing again. (Young infants do not know they can breathe through their mouth when their noses are plugged.) Amazingly, I did not panic. I had seen this before with my siblings, and I calmly told my husband we should go to the hospital because I didn't want to repeatedly nudge my baby all night to encourage breathing.

The emergency room admitting nurse complimented me on my calm demeanor. It wasn't till after the baby had been admitted to the hospital, x-rayed and placed in a tented crib that I got emotional. While certainly more difficult to deal with when it was my own child, I was thankful then that my previous experiences with my siblings had helped me not to panic. (Thankfully everyone mentioned is strong and healthy now.) Although sadly I have had to call upon this particular strength many times — staying focused and strong during difficult challenges, I feel fortunate that my parents were amazing examples of this and helped me learn this skill early on in my life.

Chapter 7: CANCER

… I would show unto the world that faith is things which are hoped for and not seen; wherefore, dispute not because ye see not, for ye receive no witness until after the trial of your faith. (Ether 12:6)

———

The story of Daniel in the lion's den found in *The Holy Bible* is world renown. This is only one episode in the amazing life of this stalwart prophet who endured so much, so far from his cherished homeland of Israel. Dragged away from Jerusalem as a child; standing up for the right against many noble kings; interpreting many dreams and writings; and finally, enduring the fearful den of beasts as an old man; Daniel embodied constant courage to his people and the rulers he served. Through all of his challenges, the scriptures show his continual faith and reliance on the Lord's guidance to overcome. Despite never being free to return home, he inspired the Babylonian rulers to respect the Jewish people, and in the future to honor the requests of Queen Esther and Nehemiah the prophet. King Darius even prayed to God that Daniel would be spared from the lions: *"Thy God*

whom thou servest continually, he will deliver thee."
(Daniel 6:16)

———

When I heard that my father had leukemia, I was shaken. He had not even completely retired from work. Cures for cancer had come a long way and I knew it was possible he could recover. I loved him dearly and life without him was unimaginable. I couldn't envision him sick either — with few exceptions he had always been up and doing. Although a bit grumpier than usual on the hard days, he exhibited the 'let's beat this' attitude he had always tackled problems with--whether it was building a garden where a jungle of weeds flourished; battling midnight flooding in a camping tent; or providing for a large family in an expensive economy. He was very pragmatic and courageous about the whole cancer ordeal. He kept his many children informed about his treatments and started a concentrated campaign to make sure his many grandchildren knew "Papa loves you".

After an intense battle of chemotherapy and a very short remission, the leukemia returned with renewed force. Although he tried more treatments, it didn't take long to see they were not working. Tall and strong, full of love and laughter, my father had always been the life of the party, but he literally began to wither before our eyes: he was barely able to stand and became very quiet. I took a trip to visit and make him some of his favorite foods, but was sad that he could barely eat them. It was obvious that he was preparing for the end: talking with special friends, listening to his favorite music, and relaxing while others read him inspirational books. Needing a break, my mother asked if I would spend the night at the house while she spent some time with my kids at the hotel and I agreed. As difficult as it was to stay up all night attending to him and talking him through the pain, our close bond and friendship deepened in ways I will never forget: walking through the valley of the shadow of death with another can be a tender and sacred experience.

Too soon he was gone. I know many have lost family and friends to cancer, but I was not prepared for the devastation of watching a beloved family member suffer so greatly and literally shrivel before my eyes. Thankfully all of my siblings were able to visit with him before his passing and some were there until the end. Although I know I will see him again and I feel his spirit near, it is a loss I still feel dearly.

Imagine my horror when the following year our younger son was diagnosed with the same cancer. I knew childhood leukemia was a bit different and more curable, but our family was stunned. It was one thing to watch my Dad suffer from afar and at the end of a life full of adventure, but to have it hit so close and to one so young was unimaginable. Immediately we embarked on an unpredictable and terrifying four-year journey. For many reasons, the doctors don't tell you much and never more than you must know at any given time. They don't want to assure you of something that may or may not happen or give you unfounded hope, but they do their best to guide you so it's easier to remain positive through a very scary ordeal. And it was frightening: they take childhood cancer patients to the edge of death to cure them and even with their assurances and confidence, every step is painful to watch and fraught with dangerous possibilities.

Luckily, they said our son would most likely live, but nine months of difficult treatments and a few years of chemotherapy, many hospital stays, a plethora of crazy medications and constant vigilance were ahead of us. He left school, received a port-a-catheter in his chest and instantly our lives centered around a mandatory schedule of hospital visits, chemotherapies, radiation, multiple medications, and the specter of life-threatening infections and fevers. Normally thin, he lost so much weight that he needed a nasal feeding tube for a few months to add extra calories each night. Although I had always been fascinated by medicine, I never expected to become an instant nurse and overnight pro at organizing and distributing dangerous medications. They even gave me a stethoscope to check the placement of the feeding tube when I needed to reinsert it at home.

Our son kept up a good attitude during the whole ordeal. Old enough to remember his grandpa's optimism during cancer, he knew a positive outlook was possible and would help him and those around him endure whatever came his way. He was kind to the doctors and nurses, patient with all the pain and procedures. He busied his mind with school work and sports stats, and although only 13 years old, he was very mature about everything. Although there were many challenging times--not keeping food down for days at a time; losing all his hair twice; loss of energy; having to avoid others and anticipated activities because of low immunities; living at the hospital for days on end multiple times--he got through it. Feeling out of sync even though the school had provided an excellent tutor, thankfully the kids were kind when he returned to school bald midway through the year. He even had one friend who printed bracelets to inspire support and make his schoolmates aware of his ordeal.

When the four years of chemotherapy were finished, his body recovered quickly. He shot up in height to 6' 3" tall and although still slim, started to resemble his teenaged buddies. He regained his energy and continues to thrive:

keeping as busy as humanly possible to try to make up for the lost years of inactivity. No one who didn't know his history would know he was a cancer-survivor, but he is a stronger, more empathetic and spiritual man because of it all. Though I would never wish this experience on anyone, it has strengthened our son in ways that cannot be measured and given him a closer bond with the Savior. It also gave him a front row seat to research science, piquing his interest in many amazing careers.

I never wanted to lose my father, and still miss him, but his amazing example of positive fortitude and faith in the Lord's plan for his life helped our whole family. It especially aided my son to endure the frightful trial of cancer when it came his way. I can say now that I am thankful for that preview of what my father endured so that in a small way, I could be prepared for what my son would experience.

Chapter 8: SORROW

*But the Comforter, **which is** the Holy Ghost, whom the Father will send in my name, he shall teach you all things, and bring all things to your remembrance, whatsoever I have said unto you. Peace I leave with you, my peace I give unto you: not as the world giveth, give I unto you. Let not your heart be troubled, neither let it be afraid. (John 14:26-27)*

———

How do you share one of the worst moments of your life and proclaim gratitude for it because it prepared you to endure a worse circumstance later? I remember being stunned when a therapist suggested that my nightmarish experience would strengthen me and others: that my example would help others see that life goes on, and one need not be a victim of circumstance. This experience and those that would follow were the impetus I had for writing this book, however I feel that specifics would not necessarily help. More importantly, those that I have aided would not give me permission to share their dark moments. I also realized I wanted this to be a book that would not shock anyone who wanted to read it.

There are many devastating crimes, events, abuse and circumstances that people endure in this life (because of their choices or those of others), but hopefully with God's help, friends, family, therapists, and time we are able to recover enough to move forward. Comparing horrible experiences is not as helpful as being compassionate to all, knowing that everyone has or will experience something that they will need help to overcome, and to pick themselves up to move forward afterwards.

In my case, three things helped immensely: therapy with a good psychologist at the outset (and other therapies throughout the years); being surrounded by positive family, friends and co-workers; and a powerful book by Dr. Susan Jeffers called *Feel the Fear and Do It Anyway* that encourages all to fight for our dreams and forgive all who might hold us back. If unable to face the person, the author recommends finding a private place to talk through your feelings and verbally forgive. I have done this and it made a big difference: anger can warp our souls and do more damage to us than to those we are angry with.

I have always been inspired by Corrie ten Boom's biography, *The Hiding Place*, and her account of how God helped her forgive one of the brutal guards from her Holocaust camp who after the war came up to her after a meeting during which she had encouraged forgiveness. She recounts how it took all her faith in God and many prayers to be able to shake his hand and forgive him.

Ever since this experience, I have come across people of all ages, including relatives and friends whose lives have been altered by the evil of others. I have been able to share with them that I understand what it is like to be a victim: that I know the heartbreak of having your safe, happy world crumble because of another's choices. I have also shared how vital it is for them to find ways to let the anger go and that therapy really helps. It has been wonderful to see how following my advice and through the comfort Christ gives, others have been able to work through the turmoil inside and heal.

There is a bond of understanding shared between those who have gone through similar difficulties and it's still incredible to me that I would be *thankful* to be a survivor. But the many opportunities when I have been able to reach out, understand, offer comfort and encouragement to others has been a true blessing. To be able to walk the path of healing with others and tenderly guide them through vulnerable moments have made me grateful that I could truly understand their pain. I now realize--even more — why our elder brother, Jesus Christ, willingly endured our pain and our sins: so he could truly know how to succor both the offended and the offender. And I am so thankful He did. My life is so much better because I asked for and received His loving-kindness through it all.

Chapter 9: PEACE

"'If it be so, our God whom we serve is able to deliver us from the burning fiery furnace, and he will deliver us out of thine hand, O king.'" And after they had been thrown into the fiery furnace and survived, King Nebuchadnezzar "saw these men, upon whose bodies the fire had no power, nor was an hair of their head singed, neither were their coats changed, nor the smell of fire has passed on them." (Daniel 3:17, 27)

"Blessed be God, even the Father of our Lord Jesus Christ, the Father of mercies, and the God of all comfort; who comforteth us in all our tribulation, that we may be able to comfort them which are in any trouble, by the comfort wherewith we ourselves are comforted of God." (2 Corinthians 1:3-4)

———

As much as anyone wants to know why difficult things happen, we must believe — as I most fervently do now — that God has a plan and wants us to succeed. I admit that some days I still ponder the reason certain events happened, why others might be transpiring in my life now, and why I must endure more, but at least I have reason to hope that there is a pattern and purpose to 'enduring to the end' and 'enduring all things'.

The Old Testament story of Shadrach, Meshach and Abednego has always been a favorite. Their unwavering faith in the Lord--that whether or not they were delivered from the fiery furnace, they would not bow to idols — is so amazing to me. I love the symbolism that we, like them, can go through the fiery furnaces of life without holding onto residual 'smoke' or 'singeing' if we will cling to our Savior, Jesus Christ, throughout the ordeal. Continually doing what we can to keep ourselves worthy and humble in order to benefit from the love and power of our Savior's atonement--which saves us, will sustain us through our darkest hours.

As I have spoken with friends during and beyond their trials, we agree that we would never wish to be in a situation where hardships constantly force us to our knees begging for Christ's constant support. But at the same time, we recognize that there is an energizing, sacred feeling of sustenance that we treasure during every moment of that closeness. Maybe that is exactly the desire of our Heavenly Father and eldest brother, Jesus Christ: to pull us close so that they might nurture us and deepen the bond between us in order to lead us home to the greatest treasure of our lives: eternal life with them.

I pray we will all strive to experience that sweet strengthening: the life-giving light, power of renewal, and revelation that can be ours as we become closer to our Heavenly Father and Jesus Christ. Be thankful for your trials: someday you will understand why they occurred and how they have strengthened you and others.

We have the freedom to choose between good or evil and how to respond to it when it affects our lives. We also have the privilege of deciding whether or not we will listen to and follow the guidance of the Holy Spirit during those experiences. Very often our choices affect other's lives and our faithful endurance will inspire them. Let us trust in the words of King Darius after the Old Testament prophet Daniel was delivered:

> *"Peace be multiplied unto you. I make a decree, That in every dominion of my kingdom men tremble and fear before the God of Daniel: for he is the living God, and steadfast for ever, and his kingdom that which shall not be destroyed, and his dominion shall be even unto the end. He delivereth and rescueth, and he worketh signs and wonders in heaven and in earth, who hath delivered Daniel from the power of the lions." (Daniel 6:25-27)*

As Jesus confirms in the book of Mark, *"with God all things are possible." (10:27)* God can safely deliver you from your fiery furnace and your den of lions too.

In telling people of my book, many have realized how past experiences prepared them and difficult events actually blessed them. What challenges have blessed you and others?

My Challenges   **My Blessings**

References

1. "desperate times called for desperate measures" is rewording of a quote assigned to the ancient Greek physician, Hippocrates.

2. Baring-Gould, Rev. S. "Gabriel's Message," a Basque Christmas folk carol. (arranged by Pettman, Edgar, 'Modern Christmas Carols' 1892. Weekes & Company.)

3. tenBoom, Corrie with John & Elizabeth Sherrill. <u>The Hiding Place</u>. Guideposts and Chosen Books, 1971.

4. Jeffers, Dr. Susan. <u>Feel the Fear and Do It Anyway.</u> Ballantine Books, 2007.

(Cover picture courtesy of JC Penney portraits digital purchase.)

Author's Info

Raised in the Manoa valley of Honolulu, Hawaii, 20 years and 7 siblings provided numerous adventures. At Brigham Young University-Laie, I earned a Theatre Associate degree while lifeguarding at the pool, served a mission to Denmark for the Church of Jesus Christ of Latter-day Saints and eventually earned a Bachelor's degree in English from BYU-Provo where I met my wonderful husband. After a lovely wedding and luau in Hawaii, we moved to Indiana, Colorado, and then Washington State — green, humid and almost as beautiful as Hawaii. Eventually blessed with four amazing children, we are thrilled at all they have accomplished in their lives.

As a disclaimer, I realize not every trial in life will be welcome: growing is painful. As lovely as C.S. Lewis' parable (recounted in his amazing work, *Mere Christianity*) of the cottage being turned into a castle is, the 'knocking about' comes at a price — I hope this book helps you see that it can be worth it. I am still trying to remind myself of this as life continues to throw challenges my way.

I have always wanted to write a book, but I never imagined it would be non-fiction. Gaining confidence while helping to edit the inspirational Live in the Q by M. Forsyth emboldened me to finish this book: an inspiration during 'Time Out for Women' in Portland, OR. I'm glad to be done after years of repeated promptings to get this published, so there's more time for swimming, word puzzles and reading fiction!

www.ingramcontent.com/pod-product-compliance
Lightning Source LLC
Chambersburg PA
CBHW060538030426
42337CB00021B/4323